THE UNIVERSITY OF

# Rules and Standards

by the same authors

**Introducing Advocacy**
**The First Book of Speaking Up: A Plain Text Guide to Advocacy**
ISBN 978 1 84310 475 9

**Listen Up! Speak Up!**
**The Third Book of Speaking Up: A Plain Text Guide to Advocacy**
ISBN 978 1 84310 477 3

**Advocacy in Action**
**The Fourth Book of Speaking Up: A Plain Text Guide to Advocacy**
ISBN 978 1 84310 478 0

of related interest

**Advocacy and Learning Disability**
Edited by Barry Gray and Robin Jackson
ISBN 978 1 85302 942 4

**Exploring Experiences of Advocacy by People with Learning Disabilities**
**Testimonies of Resistance**
Edited by Duncan Mitchell, Rannveig Traustadottir, Rohhss Chapman, Louise
Townson, Nigel Ingham and Sue Ledger
ISBN 978 1 84310 359 2

**Advocacy Skills for Health and Social Care Professionals**
Neil Bateman
ISBN 978 1 85302 865 6

**ISPEEK at Home**
**Over 1300 Visual Communication Images**
Janet Dixon
ISBN 978 1 84310 510 7

**ISPEEK at School**
**Over 1300 Visual Communication Images**
Janet Dixon
ISBN 978 1 84310 511 4

# Rules and Standards

## The Second Book of Speaking Up:
## A Plain Text Guide to Advocacy

## John Tufail and Kate Lyon

Jessica Kingsley Publishers
London and Philadelphia

First published in New Zealand in 2005
by People's Advocacy Network

This edition first published in 2007
by Jessica Kingsley Publishers
116 Pentonville Road
London N1 9JB, UK
and
400 Market Street, Suite 400
Philadelphia, PA 19106, USA

www.jkp.com

**Library of Congress Cataloging in Publication Data**
A CIP catalog record for this book is available from the Library of Congress

**British Library Cataloguing in Publication Data**
A CIP catalogue record for this book is available from the British Library

ISBN 978 1 84310 476 6

Printed and bound in the People's Republic of China
by Nanjing Amity Printing
APC-FT4808-2

'To teach a man how he may learn
to grow independently, and for himself,
is the greatest service
that one man can do another.'
Benjamin Jowett

# Contents

# 1. Why We Need Rules and Standards

## Rules

In the **first book of speaking up** we talked about what advocacy was and the different types of advocacy there are. Now we are going to discuss the things that we need to know if we are going to be good advocates. It might be a good idea if we started by talking about rules.

- We all live by rules of one kind or another.

- Rules help us get along together.

- They help stop abuse.

- They help keep us safe.

**They tell us that there are some things that you MUST do and some things that you must NOT do!**

Remember, there are some simple rules about making your own rules:

Rules are meant to help people and keep them safe.

Rules should not harm people.

Rules should never be made that treat one group of people as if they are better than another group.

Rules can be made to stop one group of people harming another.

Rules should be simple enough for everyone to understand.

All rules must be necessary. Never make a rule unless it is definitely needed.

 Rules should be agreed to by everyone they affect.

Rules don't work if there are too many of them.

## Standards

Advocacy has to work by rules. Advocacy has to have standards as well.

**Standards are about doing things well.**

When you have standards it means everyone has to do things well. They have to reach a certain standard. So standards are a type of rule.

Standards can either be laid down by someone like a government or a professional body.

Or they can be agreed among a group of people doing the same thing.

In England advocates decided it wouldn't be the right thing for them to be told how to do their job by the government. This was because the government is a provider and buyer of services. Advocates often have to ask the government questions. They sometimes have to tell the government it is wrong and will have to change its mind.

Sometimes governments make laws that are wrong. These too have to be challenged.

**So over one hundred advocacy organisations got together and decided on their own standards.**

But first they talked with a lot of people who use advocacy services to ask what sort of standards they wanted for advocacy. They wrote down all the things that people thought that advocates should do well. They wrote down some things they thought advocates should never do.

All the things they wrote down became a list of rules and standards they called **The Advocacy Charter**.

## The Advocacy Charter

Advocacy is taking action to help people say what they want. It helps people get what they are entitled to.

Advocates and advocacy schemes work in partnership with the people they support and take their side.

Advocacy says that everyone should be treated the same and have the same rights and opportunities in life.

## Making things clear and simple

An advocacy scheme should tell everyone what they do and how they do it in a way everyone can understand. It should say how it goes about keeping to the rules of this charter.

## Independence

Advocacy schemes have to be independent. No-one who provides services or pays for services should be able to tell them what to do or how to do it.

Advocacy schemes should only work in the interests of the people they are advocating for and nobody else. They should try

and solve problems when there are disagreements between the people who provide services and those who rely on them.

## Putting people first

Advocacy schemes must always be sure that what they do is what the people they advocate for actually want. Advocates should not make judgements about people or their actions or about the things they want or the things they say and believe in.

   Advocates should always share any information they get with the people they are advocating for.

## Empowerment

The advocacy scheme will speak up for self-advocacy and empowerment in what it does and the way it does it.

People who use the scheme should be able to say how much they want to be involved in their advocacy. They should have a say in how things are done and said.

Schemes will make sure that the people they advocate for can have a say in how the scheme is run if they want to. The people the scheme advocates for should be encouraged to be involved in the management of the scheme and how it is run.

## Equal opportunity

The advocacy scheme will say in writing that everyone has to be treated in the same way. This means that everyone should be given the same chances to do what they think is best for them. This is called an 'Equal Opportunities Policy'.

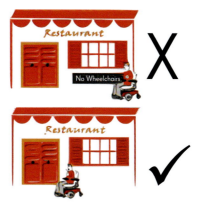

   This policy means that advocacy schemes have to try to stop unfair things happening before they start. If they think that someone is going to be badly treated because they are different, they should speak up. The scheme should make sure that its advocates work in a way that will help do this.

## Accountability

Advocacy schemes will make sure that the advocacy they give is always of a high standard. They will do this

by making sure that their work is looked at regularly by other people, including the people they advocate for. These people will tell the advocacy scheme if their work is reaching the right standard.

## Accessibility

Advocacy will be provided free to all the people that the advocacy scheme is set up to support.

The scheme will make sure that anyone can get into the building and be helped. All the publicity and rules of the scheme will say that everyone should have the same right of access to all services.

## Supporting advocates

The advocacy scheme will make sure their advocates are given the right training to make sure they can do their jobs.

Advocates will be given all the support they need. Advocates will have lots of chances to learn new skills and get better at what they do.

## Confidentiality

The advocacy scheme must treat all information about people it supports in strict confidence.

It will say this in writing so that everyone knows that this information is private and confidential.

It can only share information it has about people if a person gives permission.

If there are times when information must be shared without permission, the scheme should say when this might happen. Everyone should know about the times when this might happen.

**Complaints**

The advocacy scheme should have a policy about complaints about the scheme or about anyone working for it. This policy should be available to everyone. It should be set down in a way that is easy to understand by all people using the scheme.

The complaints policy should include a way in which someone who doesn't work for the scheme and is independent can help people complain.

This is one set of advocacy rules and standards. You can see they are quite clear and simple. They are rules that will be easy to follow and will be good for both advocates and partners.

This is just how rules should work. There is nothing to stop you setting standards for your own advocacy organisation.

## Some more about rules

The Advocacy Charter was written so that any type of advocacy service could keep to its rules. This doesn't stop advocacy schemes having other rules that will be right for what they do.

**What is important about rules for advocacy is that they should be for everyone and that everyone should have a say in how they are made up.**

An advocacy organisation shouldn't have different rules for different types of people. UNLESS there is a need to have a rule to protect a group of people who share a problem that other people don't have.

For example there might be a rule saying, 'No dogs allowed.' Then there might be another rule that says dogs that help blind people ARE allowed.

Rules are too important to be made up by just a few people. Everyone should take part in making up rules because they affect everyone.

You might want to start a group. If you do, you might want to make up some standards.

Because standards are a kind of rule, if they are going to work, everyone has to know about them and everyone has to agree about them.

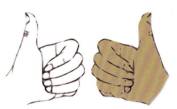

This definitely means...

**everyone who is using an advocate AND everyone who has to work with an advocate and partner HAS to know:**

- what an advocate does

- who an advocate is responsible to

- if the advocate is someone who can be trusted and respected.

Having a set of standards helps in this. But training is also very important in making and keeping standards:

- Training gives a person the confidence to speak up.

- Training is a good way of meeting other people doing the same thing. They can share things and learn from each other.

- Training tells other people that the advocate knows the job.

- Training helps the advocate avoid mistakes.

- Training teaches people things they can share with other people.

- Training helps give people an identity. They are TRAINED advocates.

- Training helps gives other people confidence in the advocate.

So training is good. Training is necessary for standards to work.

Training only really works if everyone trains advocates about the same rules. But remember – being well trained can only HELP someone be a good advocate! It can't MAKE that person a good advocate. **Being a good advocate comes from inside:**

- being honest

- believing in what they do

- working hard to achieve what they believe in

**and above all**

- respecting themselves and others.

**Sticking to THEIR rules and standards!**

# 2. Confidentiality

Personal File

People have to be able to trust their advocate.

This is because they will need to tell the advocate a lot of things that they don't want anyone else to know. These things can be anything, from telling the advocate that you don't like your carer (and why!), to telling the advocate that you throw your medication down the toilet!

So when an advocate first meets the partner they must tell the partner that anything said is private between the two. It's secret, and the advocate can only share it with someone else if the partner says so.

Personal File

**Advocates don't gossip about their partners!**

This sounds like a good idea! But it isn't quite as easy as it sounds:

- The partner might tell the advocate about something that will cause harm to the partner or others.

- Or someone like a policeman or a judge might tell the advocate, 'You must tell us what we want to know!'

If what they want to know has been told in confidence by the partner, what then?

It's difficult isn't it?

**You see, there sometimes ARE situations when an advocate has to tell someone else about things...**

...even when the things are something you learned in confidence as an advocate.

For example, say that someone had all their money stolen and someone else got the blame. Then the advocate was told in secret by their partner that that person had stolen the money.

What would they do?

They couldn't just put the money back, because the person who was blamed would still be blamed. That wouldn't be right.

Well the best thing would be to try to talk the partner into owning up. But that might not happen.

So...

**the way to avoid things like this happening is for the advocate to tell the partner, when they first meet, that there are certain things that can't be kept secret.**

A lot of people think that these things are:

- when the advocate is afraid that the partner might be in a lot of danger or at risk of harm and has to act quickly

- when the advocate knows that the partner is going to do something that might cause a lot of harm to someone else

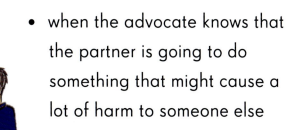

- when the advocate is ordered by a court to tell them.

If these are the rules, advocates must make sure the partner understands this. However, some people think that even this is too much.

Some people, for example, think that if advocates are not supposed to tell their partners what they can do and what they can't do, then advocates can't tell someone else (for example) that their partners have said that they are going to harm themselves.

Some citizen advocacy schemes think that there shouldn't even be any rule in advance about what you can and can't tell if you are an advocate. They think that, like friends, you should wait until something happens and then decide what is the best thing to do.

So you see...
**it is very important that everyone knows about the rules on privacy and confidentiality in your organisation. Even if the only rule is that there is no rule!**

If an advocate thinks they might have to tell somebody something that an advocacy partner has told them in confidence, they might want to discuss it with the person who is supervising them first.

Unless they really think it will do harm, they should always explain to the partner what they are going to do and why they think they have to do it. They should give the partner the chance to put things right so they don't have to break the confidence.

# 3. Duty of Care and Risk Assessment

One of the most important things advocates have to remember is that they have a **duty of care** towards their partner.

This means that an advocate should:

- never do anything that might cause harm or upset to the partner

- do everything possible to make sure the partner is not harmed.

**These two rules are what duty of care is about.**

Everyone has a duty of care towards all other people. For example, if you see some people walking along a cliff top and you know that they are walking towards a place where the cliff

is dangerous, you have a duty to tell these people about the danger.

Duty of care is particularly important in advocacy because advocates are dealing with people who might be very trusting and can be at risk. There is a special trust that the advocate's partner has in the advocate, so the advocate has a special duty of care.

This can lead to some difficult problems for an advocate.

## Making safe choices

One problem is that it is the advocate's job to speak up with the partner and not make judgements or decide for the partner what is best for him or her.

For example, say you want to take up a sport that other people think is too dangerous. Like horse riding.

'No!!' says everyone. 'It's far too dangerous. You might fall, or get kicked or the horse might bolt and hurt someone else!'

So you would never find out if you could ride a horse. It would be very bad if your advocate joined with everyone else in telling you that horse riding was too dangerous for you.

But what if the advocate supported you in persuading everyone that you should be allowed to take up horse riding and then you had a bad fall and were really badly hurt? Wouldn't that be at least as much the fault of the advocate as yourself? Wouldn't the advocate have a duty of care to tell you that horse riding was too dangerous?

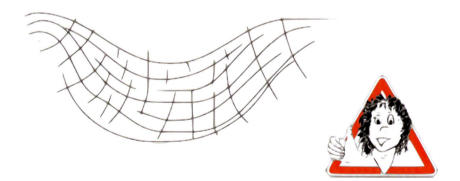

Well – this is where risk assessment comes in.

**Risk assessment is about making sure that everything is set up to keep you as safe as possible.**

It is NOT about stopping you doing things because something MIGHT go wrong. For example, horse riding is only really dangerous if it is not done properly and the right precautions are not taken. **The risk must be assessed.**

So what the advocate would do is talk with the partner and together find out what all the dangers were. Maybe asking a professional riding instructor to help. The advocate would make sure that the partner found out and understood the rules of safe riding. Together the advocate and partner would make sure things were in place to make things as safe as possible.

In the end, the advocate and his partner would work together to come to a decision about the best way to take up riding as safely as possible. If the advocate and the partner together did all this properly, then the advocate would have carried out the duty of care to the partner.

**So duty of care and risk assessment are important in helping people make choices that are safe.**

They shouldn't be used to stop people making reasonable choices.

But...

sometimes these two things are used in a way that is bad for some people. Like people with disabilities. Risk assessment can be used in a way that stops people doing what they want.

## Risk is part of life

Another problem with duty of care is that the better you are at looking after people, the greater the duty of care you

have towards others. That's what the law in most countries says.

So if a nurse helps someone who has been knocked down by a car, the duty of care on the nurse would be greater than the duty of care on, say, a shop assistant. If the person the nurse helped was harmed by the treatment the nurse gave to help him or her, then the nurse would be in a lot more trouble than if the same treatment was given by the shop assistant.

This can cause problems – a doctor and a nurse (or a care manager) become more likely to say that a person with a disability can't do something, because they are afraid that if they say that a person with a disability CAN do something, and gets hurt doing it, THEY will get into trouble!

This means that sometimes people are told they can't do something by those who are looking after them. In fact this happens a lot! This is usually because these people think the risk is too great and they will get into trouble if something goes wrong. But most people take risks in their lives – crossing a road means risk, going swimming means risk.

**Learning how to live your life to the full means that you will have to take risks!**

So risk is part of everyday life. People learn to keep the risks to a low level. They have to learn how to assess risks, how to do things safely.

But over the years people have taught themselves to think that many disabled people shouldn't be allowed to take any risks at all. When this happens, it means you can't lead a proper life. Because nearly everything you do involves a little bit of risk. Like learning to cook your own food. Or going to the shops by yourself. Or taking up a sporting activity. 'You can't do it! It's too risky!' you are told.

A lot of the time this happens because the people who are supposed to be supporting you think they will get into trouble if you hurt yourself or someone else. And maybe they are too busy to take a bit of extra time to help you assess the risk and work out how to do something the right way. The safe way.

So they play safe. That way they don't get into trouble. 'Better safe than sorry,' they say.

You don't get to do the things you want. You don't get to learn how to do things that will help you live a better life.

**So, people have to stop thinking that there is one set of rules on safety for most people and another set of rules for people who are disabled.**

**This is an important part of advocacy.**

**This is an important part of speaking up.**

## Sally's story

Sally lived in a residential home. Her legs were weak so she had to use a wheelchair most of the time.

She wanted to go horse riding. The manager said, 'No, Sally, you are too disabled.'

Sally met an advocate at a day centre. She asked the advocate to speak up for her. The advocate arranged to talk to the manager with Sally.

The manager told the advocate why Sally couldn't go horse riding. It was because two years ago a person at another home had fallen off a horse and hurt himself. So the people who ran the homes said that no-one who used a wheelchair could go horse riding.

They said that because someone had been hurt they had done a risk assessment. They decided it was too dangerous for anyone who used a wheelchair to go horse riding. The manager showed Sally and her advocate the letter that said this.

The advocate said to Sally that he didn't know what he could do. He said that the rules said it was too dangerous for Sally to go horse riding.

Sally still wanted to go horse riding so the advocate went and explained the situation to his manager.

The advocate's manager said that the rule was wrong. He said that the fact that someone in another home had fallen off a horse didn't mean that Sally couldn't ride. He said that Sally should have her own risk assessment.

Sally agreed with this. But the people who owned the homes said, 'NO! We won't change our minds.'

So Sally and her advocate wrote to the people who paid for Sally's care. These people paid for the care of most of the people in the place where Sally lived — so they were very powerful. They said Sally should have a new care plan and her own risk assessment.

The social worker in charge of the risk assessment arranged for Sally to go to a riding school to find out if she could ride safely. The riding school said that lots of people like Sally could ride, but that she would need special equipment. They didn't have the equipment.

The social worker wrote to a charity explaining that Sally needed special equipment. The charity agreed to give the riding school money for special equipment so long as they let other people with disabilities ride too. The riding school liked this idea.

Now, because Sally spoke up for herself, lots of people are learning to ride who wouldn't have had the opportunity.

# 4. Positive Risk Management

You can see from Sally's story that risk assessment is very important in getting things done. This is because when people sit down together and assess risks they can then work out how to manage risks. Things don't seem so dangerous after all.

Most of us do risk assessment every day.

When we cross a road we assess the risk by looking around us to see what traffic there is. If there is any traffic about, the wise person will look for the safest way of crossing the road – like using a pedestrian crossing wherever possible.

This is where risk management comes in.

When we have assessed a risk, when we have seen that there IS a risk involved in an activity, we have to manage it so that the risk can be made as small as possible.

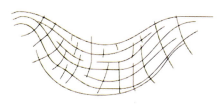

**We can't always get rid of the risk completely, but we can usually reduce it to a level where an accident is very unlikely.**

The place where most accidents happen is in the home. The place in the home where most accidents happen is in the kitchen. Everyone who works in a kitchen has to do risk assessment every day. People don't really think of it as risk assessment, they think of it as being careful.

Thinking safe!

So let's look at how risk assessment turns into risk management – and how you can't manage a risk unless you can first see that it is there!

These are some of the things you do when you go into a kitchen:

- You make sure that the floor is safe to walk on (risk assessment). It might be too slippery. There might be things you could trip over. It might be dirty so that mice and insects think it's a good place to be. And mice and insects carry lots of diseases.

- You have to think about the best way of managing things so that the risks are reduced.

- You tidy up and put everything in a safe place.

- You clean the floor. If the floor is still too slippery, you might put a mat down.

- There might be a mat already, but it's all frayed and curled up – a risk. So you change the mat.

- Then you make sure that all the surfaces you are going to work on are tidy, clean and dry. A working surface that has lots of things on that you don't need is dangerous – especially if there are dirty dishes and things. This is the **assessing** bit! Then you **manage** the risk by washing the dirty things and putting everything away in the proper place, making sure nothing is broken or worn out.

- The next thing you would do is to decide what things you will be working with and check them to see if they are safe. For example, if you are just making a cup of tea, you will make sure the kettle is safe and working properly (no frayed leads or exposed wires!), that the cup isn't cracked and that you have tea and fresh milk.

**So you can see that risk assessment and risk management is something you do every day.**

Sometimes, though, there will be people who think that you can't assess or manage risks by yourself.

Well, if you think about it this is true for everyone in some situations. For example, Sally needed to get someone who was an expert on horses to help her assess and manage the risks of horse riding. But so would anyone who hadn't ridden a horse before.

But...
what if people told you that you can't go in the kitchen because you can't be trusted to assess and manage the risks? What if someone told you that you can't take charge of your own shopping because you can't assess and manage the risks? Sometimes this happens.

It happens to young children all the time, but eventually children are trusted to do their own risk assessment and management.

However, sometimes a person might have a real problem in understanding or remembering things. Or they might never have been given the chance to do things for themselves. They might need a lot of support. When someone does need a lot of support this is what is supposed to happen:

- Those supporting such people should sit down with them and find out how much they understand and how much support they need.

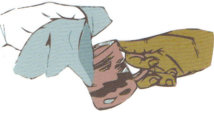

- By talking to such people they can find out how much help is needed by assessing and understanding the risks involved in each activity.

- They can then help them understand risk and how to manage it.

- They can give help when needed and give someone who needs support the confidence to do as much as they can on their own.

- They can work with people to make all the places and things around them as safe as possible.

- They can work with them in finding out the activities they want to do and how they can do these things safely.

This is positive risk management and assessment, and it is really important in helping people lead a full and safe life.

To be a good part of people's life, **risk management must be a shared thing**. The more people share and talk about things, the easier it is to understand. The more

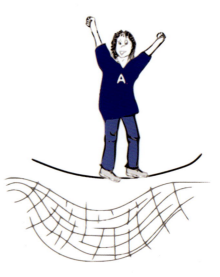

people understand something, the more they are likely to remember.

There's one more rule that all good advocates should tell themselves at all times –

**Watch yourself!**

## You could be an advocate too

You can see that being a good advocate means following a lot of rules. But if you still want to speak up for yourself and others...well, nearly everyone has it in them to be an advocate.

But before you decide this is for you, you have to ask yourself some hard questions. The thing you have to realise about advocacy is that if you are advocating for a partner, your partner is going to rely on you a lot.

Your partner is going to trust you. Your partner is going to believe that you are going to be there for him or her!

So you have to be really careful that you really WANT to be an advocate NOT an advice giver!

Lots of people like giving advice. But it takes a very special person to accept that everyone is different. And what seems good from the way you see things might not be at all good from the way the person you are giving advice to sees things. You must:

- have it inside you not to judge other people from the way you see things – this can be a very hard thing to do

- forget about YOU and think about the way your partner sees things

- have the TIME to give to your partner – it's no use saying to your partner at a difficult time that you are sorry but you, your family, your job, your hobby comes first, and that your advocacy partner will have to wait in the queue.

If you feel happy in yourself that these things aren't going to be a problem, then you can make it as an advocate.

But (there are always buts)...
**one of the most important things you have ALWAYS to remember as an advocate is that you are ALWAYS there for your partner.**

The thing is that some people have trouble with their own lives. They find it difficult coping with things that are happening in their lives.

They start thinking that they can work out their own lives by helping other people. If they can help other people, they think, they will be able to work out their own problems.

So:
- When people are depressed, they often want company and want to be valued, so they offer help to other people.

- When people are angry and feel they can't get what they want for themselves, they will try to get what they want by using other people to get a sort of revenge.

- When people are unwell sometimes they either want to strike out OR use other people to help them feel good about themselves. They do this to help themselves get better.

None of this is bad in itself – at least not always. We all have problems in our lives. Some of us have very big problems – like illnesses that won't go away – or keep coming back! But what it DOES mean is that as an advocate – someone who is going to support another person who probably has problems at least as big as yours:

**You must never use your advocacy role as a way of sorting out your own problems.**

It doesn't work! It isn't fair! It can cause harm to you and harm to the person you are working with. It is a breach of trust.

If you try to do a job when you are not fit to do that job you can get into a lot of trouble with the law! And you can get other people into trouble as well. So NEVER try to do anything when you are not fit enough to do the job safely and well.

'Please can you take over for me?'

This means not driving a car or flying an aeroplane if you are not well. And it means not acting as an advocate! Not even self-advocacy.

If you ever think you are not well enough – or strong enough – to act as an advocate, or carry on acting as an advocate:

- go and ask someone you trust and respect for advice

- explain the situation to your advocacy partner and help your partner find a different advocate if necessary

- take care of your own health so you can get better quicker

- get someone to explain the situation to the people you and your advocacy partner are working with.

You don't have to do this yourself, you might not be well enough.

Really. Think about it. We all want to be valued. Respected. It's the sort of thing that people want all the time.

But it is wrong if you want to be an advocate to let your feelings about what you need come before the needs of the person you are advocating for. Sadly, this sometimes happens! Don't let it happen to you. You have to be sure about why you want to be an advocate.

**You have to be absolutely sure that the reasons you want to be an advocate will not harm your advocacy partners.**